Preface

I am courageous, confident, wise, giving, forgiving, and beautiful. And with that being said, I am also selfish (with my time), impatient, and unpredictable.

My flaws are a part of my makeup and what makes me human. I am the first to admit my imperfections. Would you even want to be around me if it were perfect? I am a work in progress until I become *flawless*.

I can be selfish with my time. I enjoy being home alone. I often turn my phone off and can easily tune the world out. I often need and look forward to quiet moments. I relax on most weekends and take naps as much as I can. I believe time is of the essence, so I try to make the best of every awaken moment.

Patience is not one of my strong points in many situations. I sometimes want it when I want it and get disappointed when it doesn't happen. I must always remember that everything in my life is on His time and know that if I don't receive it, there could be good reasoning behind it; to always look at it in a positive light. Patience is something I work on every day. Whether it be driving, standing in line at a store or waiting for a table at a restaurant; I am easily irritated with waiting, so I make it a point to put my thoughts on other things while in the waiting.

I love this about me, but some may consider it to be one of my flaws. I am unpredictable, spontaneous and care free most of the time. I don't do much planning because I love doing things at the spur of the moment. I do better when I have one day to pack for a road trip or something needs to be completed at the last hour. I get a rush when time restraints are put on me to complete a task. I love spur of the moment things; they always seem to work better for me.

I've heard that I am too much of a risk taker, I'm too spontaneous, I'm hard to figure out, or too many times I've been indecisive... all true, but in certain circumstances. If in an uncomfortable situation, I leave. If time allows, I go. If there's something I want, I'll try it. I'm not afraid to fail. I look at failure as a way of deciding, and then knowing what is right for me. If it's not working out, whether it is a relationship or a task, I'll walk away. Sometimes walking away does not mean that you failed; it can mean that it's just not for you at that time or ever. At my age, I am not going to do much of anything that I don't enjoy doing or just simply do not want to do. Again, this goes back to me being selfish with my time. But it can also be a sign that I appreciate life more, so I'm more careful to make each moment count.

"This Is Me" embodies some of the personal chapters in my life; my struggles, heartbreaks, past relationships, family and the way I view the world. My way of releasing bad energy is to put it on paper. Today, I am a better me. My storms shaped me into a stronger, more confident being. I am a better mother, daughter, niece, cousin, aunt, sister and friend. I appreciate every wrinkle, every gray hair and extra pound or two. I love and accept the women I grew into as I am who I am... *this is me.*

Family

*If it were not for **1942** — You*

*There would not be a **1963** — Me*

*Not even a **1981** — Son*

Mommy ~ Me ~ Mike

This Is Me

The chocolate girl with low self-esteem
Always reaching at a million dreams
Timid and shy because of my speech
Believing my dreams were out of reach
Not pleased with the way that I looked
Hiding behind a pile of school books
The old men stared with hung tongues
At breast I developed so very young
Young boys smiled and some stared
Girls whispered and gave deep glares
Poetry was my way of therapy
I grew to accept & love the image of me
My big calves, brown skin, wide hips
Baritone voice, big breast and full lips
Like a soaring eagle I spread my wings
Believing that I can conquer anything
Ready to take on this big old world
Impressive for a little chocolate girl

Our Friendship

You give me this uncontainable joy that has far reached all of my expectations
Your resilience and zest for life, your compassion and good heart is breathtaking
Each day has been incredible as I am fascinated and intrigued by what's next with you
The stages of getting to know you takes me on a journey of experiencing something new
On this spectacular parallel connection that in my eyes it's a perfect unity
I rest comfortably in knowing that we are at a place right where we need to be
When all is said and done and everything's measured and falls in line
More is revealed as chains are broken and you give more of your heart and I give you mine
The spiritual connection evolves and the level of respect, love and honor surface
You begin viewing things in a different light as you become to realize your purpose
I see a different you... a better you and I marvel in the beauty and what God has next
My focus and my wants are for you to be happy and to see you at your very best

My heart bleeds love for you as I let it show through kind words and idiocy
Though it hasn't been said; it's never questioned that my heart knows you love me
Thank you for the tender moments, the laughter and for all you revealed
You've touched every emotion and kept a heart beating that needed to be healed
I learned so much about myself and I'm firm on what I need through what you assured
The day I let you in my life is the day I received a friendship that's golden... that's pure

Yours Truly,
Baby doll

These Shoes

I used to walk a lot in these familiar shoes
They held up while withstanding a lot of abuse
The heels and straps are just about gone
A reminder of scars I held on to far too long

The many times I ran fast to escape
With both heels now carrying a scrape
Times when I felt I was going to die
Running in heels five inches high

The times when I was left out in the cold
Feeling unwanted, insecure and alone
When my life was no longer in my hands
Running from the uninvited advances of a man

When I allowed myself to be disrespected
Left broken hearted from all the rejection
When I was left without a song to sing
Holding off from spreading my wings

When judged for having a baby so young
Promises broken after they had their fun
When not understanding life's lessons
And not appreciating all of my blessings

When not knowing when to say "no"
Or how to let my true feelings show
These shoes carried me thru some dark days
When the world showed me its wicked ways

I walked many miles through mud and dirt
Exhausted, humiliated and feeling hurt
I was forgiven and I know I paid my dues
So don't judge until you walked in my shoes

I hold on to them to show where I've been
The tumultuous times I once was in
Knowing I'll never go back there
My feet are more comfortable in a new pair

My First Love

How do I know it won't be like before?
When you took my love then didn't want anymore
How do I know things won't be the same?
When you left and gave someone else your name

Why didn't you see what you had back then?
A true, dedicated lover and friend
I never knew that things were so bad
I was still loving you with all that I had

How do you know right now I'm the one?
Will we be married when it's all said and done?
Will your arms be wide open whenever I fall?
Can you promise me you will give me your all?

Can I trust you again with my fragile heart?
And can I trust you whenever we're apart?
Is it because you hold on to old memories
Is why you think you're still in love with me?

After all these years, are you the man of my dreams?
Who'll be the one to exchange wedding rings?
If you honor me and give me the utmost respect
Together, we'll go on a journey you'll never forget

Tag: You're It

You're supposed to chase me until I can't run anymore
You're supposed to catch me before I hit the floor
Keep chasing me... until I run out of breath
Until I fall in your arms and I have nothing left
When you catch me; then make me your wife
And continue the chase me for the rest of your life
If you keep chasing me with charm and wit
You'll be good at this game... tag: you're it!

Grandma's Place

Southern fried chicken, collard greens
A ham hock simmering in a pot of lima beans

Roast beef and deviled eggs on chill
Potato salad with just a pinch of dill

Assorted condiments for the dipping
Gravy made from the roast beef drippings

Candied yams with a marshmallow top
Homemade lemonade or a grape soda pop

Golden brown, sweet buttered cornbread
Fresh crumbled blue cheese on a lettuce bed

Olive oil sprinkled on a cheese-toasted bun
Homemade apple pie with a hint of cinnamon

Vanilla ice cream topped with caramel and nuts
The cherry aroma from Grandpa's cigar butt

She loved her family and it showed on her face
It was always nice going to Grandma's place

The Game Of Love

He was my first love
my first passionate kiss
my heart beat rapidly
as I never felt like this

I thought no one could love me
in the passionate way that he did
I trusted him wholeheartedly
I believed every word he said

I gave him something sacred
a love that was so pure
I felt it was the only thing to do
for the relationship to be secure

Now he's was my first broken heart
after giving everything up for
one day he decided that
he didn't want me anymore

But he was my first love and
I held on for as long as I could
I kept grasping on to what was left
anything that I thought was good

With each agonizing moment
I was trying hard not to fall apart
while picking up the pieces
of my tormented, broken heart

To give yourself completely
to love with all of your might
some things you'd do to make it right
aren't always a beautiful sight

Through life you love and you learn
and sometimes you will lose
in the game of love always be careful
with the person that you choose

I Smile

When I hear his voice my heart melts

When a day without him is heartfelt

When we talk on the phone all night

When a simple touch feels so right

When I see his name on my caller ID

When I show the little girl in me

When I fumble through old photographs

When his quirkiness makes me laugh

When we both share pleasantries

The times I get weak in the knees

Knowing him has truly been a thrill

Loving him completely makes it all real

I smile at the unlimited possibilities

I smile often at you... and... me

Johnny

I knew very little about you
Yet, I carry your last name
When asked about my father
I once held my head in shame

There's not much I can say
I don't even know if you ever cared
Or if you ever loved me
Or why you were never there

I never second guessed it
Why you weren't in the home
Instead of chasing unwanted love
I chose to just leave it alone

I experienced a great love
When I had my beautiful son
I couldn't imagine leaving him
Without regret for what I'd done

I have no malice towards you
Sometimes life is just not fair
My rewards are up in Heaven
Johnny; I hope to see you there

R.I.P John Stevens

My Mr. Kellogg Man

I love it when he gives me **Sugar Smacks** and caresses my **Cocoa Puffs** because it makes me do **Trix** all over! And don't let him touch my **Fruttie Pebbles**, I feel like his **Lucky Charm** and he's my **Captain Crunch**. And I love it when he calls me **Honey Combs**, I get the **Kix** and start acting like a little kid jumping through **Froot Loops**. He is my **Total** package; some would say my **Cream of Wheat** who makes my **Toasted Oats** feel like **Golden Grahams** and I am forever his **Product 19**. Just call me **Special K** as his **Chex** is all I need to satisfy my **Rice Krispies** when yelling *Cheerios* and reciting the **Alphabets** when he touches my **Cinnabons** and I curl up like a **Raisin Bran** and his **Corn Puff** rises all over my **Frosted Flakes** then he relaxes his **Shredded Wheats** and leave me thinking about his **Nut N Honey**, so at this time I need some **Grits** or something! I tell him to stop eating those **Wheaties** as he makes my **Crixpix** melt like **Corn Flakes** and now I'm calling him my **Count Dracula** cause I feel my **Oatmeal** pouring all over. Whew, just call him my Mr. Kellogg Man!

Definition Of Love

When one feels that powerful connection
A desire, a want, an irresistible affection
An arising out of kinship or personal ties
A deep feeling when the heart won't lie
Patience; emotions filled with a strong fire
An overpowering attraction with insatiable desires
Intimacy felt for someone familiar and dear
A deep gut feeling without doubt or fear
Unselfishness, loyalty, a genuine concern
A pulsating feeling, a hunger, a yearn
An undeniable feeling, a compassionate touch
A passionate kiss, a pleasurable rush
A liking, a nervousness that melts the heart
An understanding of; until death do us part
~Love

To My Son

They said breathe, I breathed
they said push, and I pushed
then I heard you cry
and I felt no more hurt
They said congratulations
you have a beautiful little boy
and that was the beginning
of this everlasting joy
An unexplainable love
that's instant from the start
an overwhelming emotion
that fills up the heart
My prayers asked to God
to be the best I could be
as this child; *my child*
was in need of me
As the years went by
I saw you making your way
and I knew my little boy
would leave home one day
I was there to help you through
I've always extended my hand
I watched in amazement
as you grew into an upstanding man
I'll always be here for you
a mother's job is never done
I love you with all that I have
you are my precious son (Michael Miller)

I'm Good

To my first love who I gave my virginity to
You didn't stay as long like I hoped you would
But I forgive you and wanted you to know that...
I'm good   (RL)

To my son's father who left us out in the cold
You never did right by us like you know you should
Through it all, I grew stronger so please know that...
I'm good   (MM)

To the ex that never believed in me or in us
Your words cut, but helped me get out of the hood
I'm glad you get to see the phenomenal woman...
I'm good   (KI)

To the friends that were there for just a season
Soulless, taking from me all that they could
I still have mad love for you and no matter what...
I'm good

To those who beat me down with your cruel words
I was hurt, but I'm not defeated and tall, I stood
It taught me some valuable lessons, so...
I'm good

Lady In The Mirror

As I stare and ruminate about my life while examining my reflection
Is it just a mere image of what I dream to be?
Or am I trying to be something that I'm not for fear of rejection?

Feelings so overwhelming permeate deep into the core of my being
As I study to make sense of the person before me
Stripped of the uncertainty; the true lady is what I am now seeing

Why am I afraid to show my flaws and the apparent imperfections?
For I am a human being as my flesh proves this
I am always going to make mistakes and fall short of perfection

I wear my scars and battered heart underneath this hard exterior
So much so, that the true me is not always shown
I must remember that when I'm whole I become more inferior

When challenged or faced with adversity; each layer is peeled
A brazenly strong person emerges, standing tall
When touched delicately then my candid heart will be revealed

I can rejoice during the times God allows me to trample through the fire
Even with burnt feet and the strong aroma of ash
I am more than a conqueror for He gives me what my heart desires

The lady in the mirror has blemishes that in time are sure to heal
Still in the process of accepting and loving who I am
I must infuse in my mind that I am beautiful and to always keep it real

Menopause

What is this?
What's making my mood go so low?
Making me want to literally chew nails
And tell everyone where they can go?

Is this even my body?
Because it's doing crazy things
I'm having my own little private summers
Always bloated along with mood swings

Not again!
Everyone is getting on my nerves
I'm sweating in the middle of winter
Dripping from each and every curve

Can you believe this?
One minute I'm up the next minute... down
I never know how my day will begin
One minute a smile next minute... a frown

Here we go again
That will be me if you hear a grunt
Mother Nature gives me no breaks
It's that dreadful time of the month

Gotta love us!
We really are as nice as we can be
It's just when old age approaches
You better not mess with me!

Anybody's Daughter

You see the torn, dirty clothes with the colors fading
You know the street corners where she'll be waiting

The once pearly whites are now a stained brown
You see her running frantically from town to town

The real loud voice, almost always a holler
Hustling... trying to make a fast dollar

Many stare believing there's no hope
They can sadly see her hanging from a rope

The pan handling and her constant beg
The dirty men in and out of her bed

Because of her the family is shamed
Her chosen life style damaged their name

She never worries that she could be harmed
Selling her body to put a needle in her arm

Many may think she's the scum of the earth
But to some mother she's a beautiful birth

What you see is not what her mother's seeing
Her baby girl is still a precious human being

She remembers the vivacious little girl
Who had so much to offer this world

An angelic voice with a heart of gold
But many have yet to see this all unfold

We think this is not the world's concern
We keep allowing her to crash and burn

We see the ugly, but her family sees the glory
They pray for a happy ending to her story

While she prostitutes and shoots up dope
Her mother hurts, but never gives up hope

Don't judge by sending her to be slaughtered
Keep in mind that she is somebody's daughter

A Woman

The silkiness; the softness of her skin
The curviness from hip down to shin

The various styles and colors of hair
Defining lines for battles she bears

Featherlike, soft, full luscious lips
Her child bearing, firm, strong hips

Keeping her children close by her side
With an overflowing abundance of pride

Sleek, proper, full of elegance
Studious; beaming with intelligence

Wearing scars from previous wars
Arms always open as wide as sea shores

Years of refinement enlightens her face
Her cup runs over with beauty and grace

A loyalty that bears no end
An honest, sincere, reliable friend

Proudly uplifts the love of her life
The epitome of a bona fide wife

A woman of substance, a valuable gem
Keeps her identity while following him

Behind every good man there she stands
Together they beam with clutched hands

It's not easy as she runs a daunting race
Persevering while keeping a steady pace

A woman of substance, essence of truth
She becomes flawless after paying dues

Kiss Me

Kiss my face
… my lips
… my ear
… my cheek
Touch every emotion until I'm restless… exhausted and weak

Rub my shoulders
… my neck
… my arms
… my hair
Until I'm so relaxed and I exhale… while taking in fresh air

Massage my temples
… my back
… my feet
… my shin
Take me wherever you need me to go… then kiss me again

My Fairy Tale

We women grew up reading about it
The glass slipper that was the right fit
How they lived happily ever after
We believed and wanted all of it

The handsome knight in shining armor
Coming on a beautiful galloping horse
No fights were ever revealed
And you never heard of divorce

We lived in this fantasy world
Anticipating meeting our perfect prince
First the ring, a big wedding, children
The house with a white picket fence

We played out the role so many times
We planned weddings in our head
Most times reality is not as thought
So the fairy tale dream is dead

We pretend at times we're okay
We try to enjoy date after date
We begin to lower our standards
Then stop looking for our soul-mate

We're familiar with the game out there
Nothing is what we always dreamt of
The fantasizing is fading
We just about given up on love

But I still believe in fairy tales
And because I still believe in this
Until I meet my "Mr. Right"
How many more frogs will I have to kiss!!!

Attitude

Baby...

Because I speak to defend myself
And won't allow you to push me around
Every time we try and talk things over
You say my tone is too loud

If you want to be head of our home
Show me what a good man should do
Be a good father, husband, and provider
Because this is not all about you

When you treat me as your equal
I won't make you feel less of a man
I have an opinion, objections and a voice
You should appreciate a strong woman

Not every time I open my mouth
Means that I'm trying to fight
My voice is strong and powerful
To speak up is my God given right

Boss...

Why is it when I show my frustrations
I am viewed as another one of *"those"*
I work hard under tough conditions
And sometimes I have my woes

I believe that you'd rather not handle
Any strong woman from my race
You'd rather for me to be silent
And to always know my place

But being silent would not be beneficial
To those behind me or yet to be born
You get to fuss and air your frustrations
So understand; my voice will carry on

I was given something so precious
That you or no man can take away
And sometimes before I speak to you
I have to get on my knees and pray

Friend...

If you can't handle me being honest
And you quiver whenever I speak
Accept me as I am, my friend
I've never been soft or meek

I've always been one to speak out
Being without words is not what I lack
It worked when you were in trouble
When I stood up and had your back

So now you want me to be quiet
Or only speak when I'm spoken to
Should I keep my advice & knowledge?
Will my being silent then work for you?

You view it as me being opinionated
I see me speaking up as being strong
Our mothers and their mothers didn't dare
So how can you view it as being wrong?

Women...

You always say to me you don't get it
And believe me, I do understand
Most women allowed husbands to rule
They just shut up and followed the man

A lot of times I truly speak in love
Then there's times when my tongue is raw
If you and others can't handle it
Then tell Congress to make a special law

Don't view it as me having an attitude
When I open my mouth with words
Whether you like, dislike or embarrassed
My voice will always be heard!

I Need You

I can cook, clean, and go to school
I can work and make my own money
I can do most anything I want to do
But it's not much without you, Honey

I can replace a light bulb and use a tool
I can take out the trash and paint a wall
I can change a tire on a car or truck
But I'm not trying nor want to do it all

I proved I can raise a successful young man
I can purchase a house with my own credit
But coming home to an empty bed
Is not what I want anymore, so I get it

I'm not trying to be a super woman
And I'm not trying to run the show
I need you right here beside me
So together we can prosper and grow

For years I was wearing the pants
But that's not what I'm built to do
I need to relax and be a little softer
And show you that I do need you

Who's Loving Me?

I thought you loved my swaying hips
My baritone voice; my luscious lips

My waist length braids, my cocoa skin
The confidence I hold within

My many shades, my voluptuous size
I thought I still was the Black man's prize

Am I no longer your African Queen?
Your rock, your strength; your everything?

But you're no longer here for me
And because of this I lost my identity

Suddenly I struggle to be a size four
My hair and nails aren't mine anymore

I see you dating all over the place
And yet I chose to stay in my race

Still attracted and still loving you
Still accepting all the wrong you do

Trying not to believe for the millionth time
That a good black man is hard to find

Rustling with thoughts of what's wrong with me
When you look, tell me what do you see?

A diamond, a ruby, or a rare gem
Who will love, cherish, and honor him

Statistics shows more black women are alone
Because our black men are leaving the home

Whether it's to another or jailed for a crime
Their leaving their women and kids behind

I want you to know I still believe in you
I'm your biggest supporter in whatever you do

Our structured bodies, strong hearts and souls
Is what keeps our race alive and whole

I understand and know the suffering you endure
I know the reward for us that God has in store

The connection that only comes through genetics
Is the most sacred union that comes if you let it

But until you come back, I'll wait patiently
But it poses the question; "Who's loving me?"

This Thing Called Life

The next time you decide to complain
Be mindful of someone else's rain

Ever watch a homeless person try to stay warm?
Have you held an infant who was still born?
Ever sit with someone who was terminally ill?
Ever needed to take more than several pain pills?

Are you blind, deaf, and/or unable to speak?
Do you only have one pair of shoes for your feet?
Did you not have enough money to pay your bills?
Are you an innocent man who just ate his last meal?

Do you suffer from chronic, debilitating pain?
Shall I go on or still listen to you complain?

Have you watched a person as they lay and die?
Have you watched your child shoot up to get high?
Are you a parent who lost their only son at war?
Got AIDS from someone out to even the score?

Ever made a decision to end someone's life?
Or a man that after 50 years had to bury his wife?
See the face of a child at an adoption center?
Waiting for a family, but no one ever enters?

After my message, now you make the call
Do all your problems now seem too small?

Mommy

Your love has no restraints or boundaries
It's unconditional, authentic and true
It's not complicated; it's always there
That's what I most love about you

You showed me things through your eyes
So I am more clear and able to see
And most of all, my precious mother
Thank you for allowing me to be "me"

Dedicated to my mother – Barbara Stevens

He Said; She Said

He said;
I don't know if you're ready for me
I know right now you think that I'm the one
You see, I been through some things in my life
And I don't believe that my struggle is done

At my age I'm still paying child support
And I'm still responsible for two other lives
To make ends meet I work long hard hours
I still communicate and support my ex wives

There are many days when I feel too beaten up
And I shut down and just want to be left alone
My occupation takes me from state to state
So most communication will be over the phone

My heart's been broken one too many times
I don't know if I can even do this thing right
I keep climbing and climbing the mountain
But the mountain is winning the fight

It's been so long since I met someone like you
Who literally took my breath away
Who shows me a pure, undeniable love
And makes me smile everyday

My heart knows you're the one for me
But then I'm still reminded of all my strife
I'm conflicted with doing this all over again
Yet, I want you to become my wife

I don't want to put you in a position
Where you have to bear my storm
As much as I hate to admit this
I think we both should move on

Right now my life is just too complicated
And I don't know where to fit you in
I'm not ready to make any kind of commitment
Except for us to continue as friends

She said;
I understand what you're going through
And I appreciate what all you've said
And I know you want to put dating on hold
Because you need time to clear your head

You see the peace that I have in my life
But you don't know of the battles I had to fight
So trust me when I say that I understand
But know that God can, and will make it all right

Through all your hurt and the stained heart
And the times you try to play it tough
I see the genuine, kind hearted, true man
I can clearly see my diamond in the rough

My heart tells me that you are the one
So when I love, I love with all of my being
And because you are not used to a love like mine
You don't trust in the things that you are now seeing

Because of the conflict you had to deal with
It's made you bitter and unable to trust
Your focus is only on your tribulations
So you miss the beauty of the two of us

In time I know that this too shall pass
And the great man will finally surface
And through the guidance of the Lord
You'll understand and know your purpose

I'll be there while you climb your mountains
And I promise to do whatever I can
This will strengthen, mold and shape you
Into a God fearing and a better man

He said;
In the midst of what I've been going through
My troubled eyes can clearly see
That God picked through all the great women
Then He perfectly sent you to me

He told me that He keeps His promises
When I was on my knees to pray
He said someone will enter your life
And make all the old things go away

He told me that she will be refined
And polished like an old cherished flute
And together we'll be happy and blessed
With power, a commitment and youth

I didn't understand what I was hearing
For I wanted to stay focused on all the pain
I couldn't believe someone like me
Would have blessings pour down like rain

Someone to love me without measure
I just could not see or comprehend
The fear took me to a dark place
Where I thought we'd be better at being friends

I'm listening as you're talking
And the words are like notes in my ear
Of a wholesome, sweet love song
That you ever could imagine or hear

She said;
It's good that He is talking to you
For His word is like pure gold
In order for you to prosper in life
You must listen and do as you're told

Through the fear, uncertainty and unknowing
I already know what you're capable of
I give you my solid commitment of loyalty
And the strong allegiance of my love

Fathers

He says he's not bothered by it
But I know the pain has to run deep
I know there's emptiness in his heart
And there are secrets he will keep

The main character is missing
When he looks at his family portrait
The pain sometimes cuts like a knife
The home was supposed to be his fortress

When he's with friends & their families
I see the look of envy on his face
When he sees fathers with their sons
I know sometimes he feels out of place

I did the best I could do as a mother
Raising a son to become a man
I know there are things he's missing
Being raised by only a woman's hand

His father was granted a second chance
The two together is how it should be
I hold no hatred for his father
Because of the Christ in me

But men, stay with your children
Or even help a boy who's lost his way
They desperately need your guidance
Grab a young man's heart today

My America

What is this place? America
The place I call my home
The place of hopes and dreams
A place where free men roam

My ancestors were forced here
To be of the slave master's needs
Treated like vicious animals
To a land not theirs for keeps

How did they feel about America?
Made as spectacles, hung from trees
Whipped badly upon their backs
Mocked as they fell to their knees

Unable to vote or fight in wars
Stripped of their God-given rights
Silenced by the devil's hand
Incapable to stand up and fight

Family's separated, babies killed
Each day was lived in fear
Blood remains on many hands
Without repenting, without care

We are still fighting for respect
As racism continues to live on
Abe Lincoln freed the slaves?
Then a new racism was born

Are we really free in America?
Are we equal and treated fair?
Not judged by the color of skin
Have we finally gotten there?

Equality was set in position
Allowed to work, but in disgrace
Laboring hard, but underpaid
More challenges for us to face

Considered second class citizens
Only to sit on the back of the bus
Still searching for another strong leader
Black America - what happened to us?

If the riots did not happen
I wonder today where we would be
I had no choice but to make this home
America ... do you accept me?

Are our fore fathers singing praises
Or are they turning in their graves
When they see the new America
Will they lift the flag to wave

I ask again; America
As we walk in the land of the free
Are we on an even playing field
In every way treated respectfully

God says to love thy neighbor
As He so loves you
Our main focus should be equality
America, God Bless You!

Beautiful Woman

Woman; you are so beautiful
My wondrous creation by far
As stunning as my garden
Bright as a shining star

I created you from Adam's rib
With so much love and pride
I made him your protector
To stand right by your side

You have the greatest ability
The joyous gift of giving birth
You're the mother of my children
You help to populate my earth

I knew your heart would break
I knew you'd shed many tears
I gave you irrefutable strength
To persevere for many years

At times you'll fight battles
And wear the emotional scar
But this will help shape you
Into the precious gem you are

For I knew that through it all
Remarkably, your light would shine
Woman; you are so beautiful
You are a daughter of mine

Our Daughter's Role Models

Destined to be role models for young girls
You see them on the cover of Vogue magazine
They show off their size 2, flawless figures
And our daughters strive to be lean

Swimsuits show off their ribs and collar bones
Rated and praised for being a perfect ten
Earning millions and trips to London, Paris
So our daughter's motivation is to be thin

They are viewed as having the glamorous life
The luxury of travelling all over the world
Affording flats in Europe and condos in the US
Mesmerized and in awe are our little girls

They don't know the sacrifices that were made
Rarely hear of what happens behind the scenes
The struggle to always stay young and on top
The silent cries or the heart wrenching screams

At a tender age they're considered washed up
Yet they've barely lived half of their lives
They are admired mostly for their outer beauty
Men marry and flaunt them as trophy wives

The younger they are the fresher the face
Approached by the pedophiles and thugs
Their lives are not as glamorous as it seems
A high percentage hide behind alcohol and drugs

We need to hear more of their personal stories
Of just how hard it is to be in their shoes
The eating disorders, the underage exploitation
The sacrifices and all of the unpaid dues

Bring light to more of the full figured models
Let our daughters dream and also realize
If their heart desires they can walk the runway
And they are beautiful NO MATTER THE SIZE

Thank you Tyra Banks for your changes in the modeling industry!

What A Beautiful Day

I woke up this morning... it was just another day

I hate my job, but I go to work because I need the pay

I sometimes yell in traffic and stay in the fast lane

At work I speak, but don't care to know their names

I go home, grab a bite to eat, then I watch a little TV

And before you know it the television is watching me

The alarm goes off in the a.m. again, just another day

A friend sent a text message and all it said was "pray"

I did, grabbed my keys, on my way to work I went

I moved to the slow lane; this should have been a hint

I greeted my co-workers with a hello and a grin

The day was so pleasant that I didn't want it to end

At home I called some family just to say, "I love you"

I wrote letters to servicemen; "thanks for all you do"

Before I knew it was fifteen minutes before eleven

I got on my knees and sent special prayers to Heaven

The joy and elation from being committed to pray

Makes me excited to begin another beautiful day!

So This Is Love

It surely wasn't love at first sight
Nothing about that moment felt right
The way he looked, the way he dressed
The words he spoke, I was not impressed

But I reluctantly continued the date
Convinced that he was not my mate
His conversation didn't interest me at all
But I was there and in it for the long haul

We ended the date with a simple good-bye
Once in my car I released a big sigh
This dating thing has hit a bad nerve
It's hard to find what I feel I deserve

I squirmed every time that he called
I really had no interest at all
But like a gentleman he continued to pursue
I felt being polite was the nice thing to do

He sent flowers, candies and nice cards
This made breaking it off with him so hard
Friends told me I wasn't used to the good guys
They said to open my heart and give it a try

So I relaxed and saw this beautiful man
Who was ready to put a ring on my hand
I paused, then gave him all of me
His eyes showed all that I needed to see

He treated me right, just like a queen
He showered me with beautiful things
He showed me how a real man should be
He rearranged his life to center around me

I get butterflies whenever he's near
My feelings are now bringing me to tears
I know he loves me unconditionally
I'm the one ready to get down on one knee

I'm so glad I opened my heart that day
And I didn't let this good man get away
With all of my heart I love him to no end
He's my confidant, my lover, my best friend

Such Is Life...

Her entire life was filled with sadness
She tried hard to erase the pain
And just when she thought she made it
It would pour down on her like rain
In order to handle the pressure
She stuck a needle in her vein

He lives in misery with his secret
Hiding it from family and friends
He fears he'd be ridiculed and rejected
It was at his best to just pretend
Dating and hurting plenty of ladies
Because he preferred to be with men

She married him for better or for worse
But it seemed the worst was all she got
Finding it difficult to get along
When they argued and when they fought
She soon came to the realization that
Her prince charming, he was not

He was sure to make his parents proud
He had big dreams of playing in the NBA
His world came crashing down in an instant
Learning that he had a baby on the way
Distraught, confused and angry
He chose to walk out on his family that day

It was a lot of fun while it lasted
She knew it was wrong what she did
She loved her husband when they married
But she was way too young to wed
The affair took its toll on the marriage
Her husband put a gun up to his head

He wasn't ready to be a teen father
So he left it all in his girlfriend's hands
His daughter grew up without him
And struggled at trying to understand
He sat on the back pew on her wedding day
As she was escorted down the aisle by another man

When life seems too unbearable
When you don't want to face another day
When nothing seems to go right
Get down on your knees and pray
Put all your faith and trust in the Lord
Through His promise, He will make a way

The World's Icon
A tribute to Michael J. Jackson 8-29-58 to 6-25-09

There was a time when I was amazed by it all
I was in awe by all of the glory
I bought the CD's, videos and magazines
And I was intrigued by all of the stories

He was the master of entertainment
And was appropriately titled, "King of Pop"
Even while being dragged through the mud
I never wanted the music to stop

For years he was constantly in my home
I watched my son try to emulate him
I saw the users, the liars and the naysayers
And was astonished and appalled by them

With all the bad press, the ridicule
I felt most sorry at what I was seeing
This man was brought down with such malice
Some forgot that he was a human being

Believe what you want about this icon
A person who never developed into a man
Or a person always crossing over the line
There are many things we fail to understand

The fingers that pointed at him
Tried to strip him from all of his fame
Strip him of his dignity, his manhood
Calling him everything but his birth name

They want us to remember the creepiness
The accused rapist or the drug addiction
They show pictures to constantly remind us
As they continued their crucifixion

With all the pain that he endured
His body couldn't take much more
God reached down his comforting hand
And opened Heaven's door

Thousands came out to mourn him
I saw many with disbelief on their face
I heard him called "a powerful soul"
Who brought together a human race

So in death how will he be eulogized?
What will the media now have to say?
He was the greatest entertainer of ALL TIME
You simply cannot take that away

Rest in total peace the world's icon
I hope in your final years we did you well
Your music will live on forever in our hearts
As we salute you a final farewell

The Music Lives On (Forever)

Let's go back to when music was real
The rich voices and the way it made you feel
The soulful sounds of Mr. Marvin Gaye
Earth Wind & Fire and the mighty O'Jays
Smokey was every young girls dream
The fabulous Diana Ross and The Supremes
Go further back when music soothed your soul
There was no other like him, Mr. Nat King Cole
Dizzy Gillespie sure knew how to blow a horn
Ms. Billie Holiday, a star was surely born
The beautiful Dinah Washington and Ms. Ella
The woman with the baritone voice, Ms. Della
And the man with all the beautiful looks
The magnificent sounds of the late Sam Cooke
Back then there were so many great hits
Bootsy, and Parliament and the Funkadelics
James Brown could dance and was always clean
The great ballad singer no other than Mr. Al green
Stevie, Otis, Barry White and Donny Hathaway
Isaac Hayes and Curtis Mayfield all paved the way
Gladys, Patti, Teena... no last names needed
Aretha "Queen of Soul" is how she's greeted
The greatest group ever was the Temptations
The Motown sound brought together a nation
It's refreshing to know the music will forever live on
Go ahead Dizzy, keep blowing your horn!

All For Love

I finally opened my eyes to see the light
    Things weren't like I thought they were, not quite
You hold back, only allowing to reach a certain height
    Afraid of love so you don't want to get close; you fight
While I'm loving you with every fiber and all of my might
    I need closure because I understand it's just not right
I see you doing little things sometimes out of spite
    I'm ready to get off this roller coaster and finish this plight
But I keep remembering what you said last night
    The question is; I guess you did it all for love... right?

A Gem

Someone who will shine on you when you feel the rain is never ending

One who will catch your tears when your fragile heart needs mending

Someone who will uplift you and have opened arms whenever you fall

Someone who will fight with you, but has your back in spite of it all

It's hard to find that someone who will ride with you through thick and thin

We all get one in our lifetime... the most precious, rarest, irreplaceable, treasured gem

Good-bye

~Hi baby, please pick up the phone
I want you to know that I know I was wrong
And I imagine you're going through hell
I don't want to leave all of this on voicemail
I'll try calling later in an hour or two
Baby, I really need to talk to you

~It's me again; it's a quarter past ten
I guess I need to face that it's the end
I'll leave a brief message to let you know
That I'd like one last minute before we let go
I was a fool to disrespect you in that way
And I know there's a heavy price to pay
I have no excuse… no reason or rhyme
I'll call you back baby another time

~Hi baby, it's been a week and I'm really missing you
I'm trying to figure out what I need to say and do
I was used to walking away when times were rough
And hiding my feelings meant that I was tough
But since losing you I'm hurting inside
It's hard to admit… you know a black man's pride
We'd rather suffer than to say what we really feel
Thinking it's best when we hide and conceal
I'm ready to open up with all my confessions
And suffer the consequences for my transgressions

Because I know you are the best thing for me
And I'm sorry it took me so long to see
But I promise you if you give me another chance
I'll cherish you and I'll even save you the last dance
I'm smiling because dancing is what you love to do
I'll step up, be a man and give everything to you
I'll end this call, but to make it short and sweet
Please call me back, let me know when we can meet

~Hi baby, I never knew we'd be apart for so long
I talked to my mother, she knows I done you wrong
She said the worst I could do was to not apologize
And to stay true by revealing all of my lies
I cheated because I thought I needed something else
Maybe something different, only thinking of myself
The ugliness of betrayal got the best of me
And caused me to lose you and my family
I miss you baby and my little lady too
Please tell her daddy says "I love you"

~Hey Baby, I know someday our paths will cross
I been going to counseling to deal with this loss
With so much guilt inside I knew I needed help
And I'm finally learning to work on myself
I like... no, I love the new me... I really do
I had to recover before coming back to you

I was not proud of the life I was living
It's good to know that God is forgiving
And I know one day you'll forgive me too
My heart will never stop beating for you

~Hello Baby, I just completed six months of rehab
I'm looking at life through clear eyes, I might add
I see my faults and all my shortcomings
I'm ready to face all of them instead of running
See, if I set a fire I got to put out the flame
And stand up and admit when I am the blame
I know time will allow us to be together again
Or maybe allow us to reconnect as friends
Thanks for the pictures of my little girl
You and my daughter are truly my world
When I stepped out on you I put my family at risk
There's no way on God's earth that I'm proud of it
I know soon you'll see the better man I've become
And then you and I can unite as one
I've come so far from my wicked past
All I have now are our old photographs
But in due time I know I'll see your face
I pray that it's His will and His forgiving grace

~Baby, I cannot believe it's been a year already
I've come far, but still sometimes my heart is heavy

See, I knew I'd have to pay for my mistakes
But I sometimes question just how long it will take
You know the old me, so I know this may sound odd
But I've been doing a lot of talking with God
I'm a saved man and could never be happier to admit
Following the rugged road is something I'm done with
I'm also celibate, can you believe that?
He's changed my life and I see the huge impact
My body's been cleansed, my mind's at ease
Now when you meet me I know you'll be pleased
I was doing it all for you, but now it's for me
I now can stand up and take care of my family
I'm doing well and I hope you're doing the same
Today I'm ready to give you my last name
I'll never mislead you, I'm honest and true
Until we're brought back together, God bless you

This Is Me Again

I often give too much of myself which often results in a difficult, painful end
Made sacrifices trying to always be there for everyone including family and friends

Left with the heavy load of carrying other people's problems and crosses
Left out of the equation when I gave my heart so I'm left with counting up my losses

I've felt pain in places where one would never even imagined or think of
Had many sleepless nights of me pretending not to still be hurt and in love

I thought the impossible was still within my reach when stretching out my hand
I tried finding purity in a commitment in a good but an unsaved man

I still run in circles and laugh at some of my excellent but crazy ideas
Because of it I know how love, disappointment, hurt, and rejection feels

I am grateful for the gifts God's given me and thankful for storms I went through
All that has happened has shaped me into a better me so I can be better for you

I'm a better mother, daughter, sister, cousin, auntie, niece, great aunt and friend
I have loved many, lost a few, forgave and been forgiven
… this is me again!

I Believe In You and Me

The last few years have been a rollercoaster ride
The heaviness at times makes it feel like a blur
I'm so used to fighting to keep a relationship
That I thought that was just how things were

One day I pray to meet someone special
Who'll change my soul, my heart and mind
Who'll validate that it is not hopeless
That true love is not impossible to find

The little girl that's still inside of me
That was once struggling to find her way
Fondly recalls the days of fantasizing
When her Prince Charming came her way

The guy who loved and protected her
As he did with all the women in his life
The guy who was not afraid to step up
And make her his beautiful wife

Who desired and embraced the challenges
Admired the strength that she holds
Who is patient through her shortcomings
And excited about how the journey will unfold

And I still prays for him come my way
Many nights as I am down on my knees
I'll open my heart to let you inside
Because I'll believe in you and me

It may not have been said often, but it goes without saying; I love my siblings.

Rest in sweet peace Kimberly Joy Stevens

There was always that fear of getting old. I worried about turning 40… then 50; it just seemed too big of a number. It reminded you that you already lived more than half of your life. All the fun was gone and it was now time to get more serious about every aspect of your life. Going forward, every decision was going to be more crucial and mistakes will have a higher price to pay. I know; I was foolish to think that getting old meant you lay still and wait to die.

But now that I surpassed both those numbers mentioned, I realize that the fear came from focusing on the number and not on the quality of life that's attached to each decade that you live. I'm blessed to have made it to a milestone where I can say that I've now lived for more than half of my life expectancy. I'm in relatively good health, I have my sane mind and I have wisdom beyond my years. I am the second living generation of my family tree; born to John and Barbara Stevens. It seems like yesterday when I had great and grandparents before me. Now, I am almost one of the oldest of my immediate family tree.

My promise is to tell my younger generation of nieces, nephews and a host of second and third cousins about their heritage and the legacy of the "Hill" family.

This section has poems written for friends and family. My feelings are always written on paper, so I am proud to share my sincere feelings with you.

Pam,

At the time when you met me
I was going through a lot of mess
Things that made me sad and afraid
So you didn't get to see me at my best

Confused, battered and lonely
Not knowing my safe place
Then God sent me an Angel
You were my saving grace

You took me in without complaint
This gave me time to be out on my own
And grow into the person I am today
And to know that I am not alone

I can remember the nights we talked
It helped me to better understand you
And we shared some private stories
That's when the bond between us grew

As wonderful as you were to my child
I know there has been so much joy
Through photos, I see your blessings
In the eyes of your two boys

I believe that when you love someone
That the love for them never parts
My love for you still lives in me
It lives in this beating heart!

"I cherish you Pam."

Trisha,

I got the chance to really know you
Through family and close friends
And what I most like about you
Is there's no fakeness, no pretend

Everyone has a buildup story
Of how life took us through some things
We grow from our testimonies
Before we accept our Angel wings

The last time that I saw you
It was as if in our younger days
Where we sat around the table
And just talked the night away

Girl, I see us on Burrell Street
Up all night playing cards
To not see Donna, Gramps and "Ma"
Sometimes it is so hard

It's good to see all of us connected
Because I look at you all as family
We may not talk all the time
But I'm here if you ever need me

I have so many fond memories
From Pittsburgh to VA
I'll always cherished our times
We both have certainly found our way!

Always love for you Trisha!!!

Alonzo,

Sometimes life hits us hard
And we get lost along the way
And no one can control our thoughts
And there's no words left to say

Sometimes we are picked up
And still we chose our path
Thinking we are better off
While caught up in the devil's wrath

Then something someone says to us
Finally helps us to see
That we, too, can reach for the stars
And be all that we can be

Still hesitant to fully express yourself
Still reminded of your past
But know that God is a forgiving God
When old friends are quick to cast

I am so proud of you, Alonzo
And I see further than what you know
I see so much greatness for you
I see divine pasture for you to go

Keep doing your thing cousin!!! Love you!!!

Lena,

Striking, as a bolt of lightening
flashing through the night sky
Confident, as a mother lion
watching over her pride
Pretty, as a picture of perfection
hanging as valued art
Lovely, as a flawless diamond
that can't be sold or bought

Funny, loving, bright and free
this is what you look like to me

I see in those eyes that you've
come out of some things
And some one important
took you under their wings
Loved by many, trustworthy
dedicated & honest, too
In that smile and those eyes
Is how I can write about you!

You are beautiful Ms. Lena

Stardom,

Such a beautiful, vivacious young lady
You have made your mother so proud
I can see her smiling upon you
And standing shouting out loud
That she appreciates the time God gave her
To give you just enough of what you need
To continue your journey in her honor
As to see you blossom and succeed
Whenever you feel that familiar presence
Know that a precious Angel is around
As God will NEVER forsake or leave you
He will keep you on solid ground!!!

"We must meet again soon Star"

Jonnise,

When I first heard you sing a song
I was mesmerized and in awe
I grew to see the gentle person
and just how beautiful you are
I remember us walking to school
I remember you holding my hand
I felt that sisterly connection
that only you and I would understand
I wanted so much to be like you
So your life I tried to rehearse
Each stage that I enjoyed with you
I mimicked every chapter, every verse
Your dance is like a beautiful swan
Your spirit is that of gold
Your eyes hold buried treasures
Of epic stories that are untold
I captured a lot of our moments
Of two talented kids in younger days
One embraced us with your stories
And captivated us through her plays
Remember the house on Garfield
That's where my memories begin
Cousins, who were so much more than that,
We are, by choice, great friends
My love for you is immeasurable
And held high within my heart
As I look back on our yesteryears, I see
Those two little girls who will never part

When I see "The Color Purple" I think of you Nise!

Alyce
"Our Little Kitten"

My memories about you
Are from many years ago
The sweetest little girl
You'd ever want to know

I cherish the talks we have
And that I got the chance to see
The intelligent, inspiring woman
That you have grown to be

We share a similar story
Of strength, determination and drive
Accepting where we are in life
Filled with a vast amount of pride

Always helping others
Standing behind the scene
Often looking in from a distance
Taking in what it all means

You're admired in so many ways
Trusted far beyond what the eye can see
I am honored to have you in my life
Grateful that you are my family

I love you infinity Kitten!

LaChar,

I fondly remember the day you were born
And the glow in your mother's eyes
As I knew how much she welcomed you
With the highest amount of pride
You were such a blessing and joy
And you still are to this day
Your mother's unending love for you
Has helped guide you in the right way
LaChar, to us you are so precious
And no matter if I'm near or far
I am proud of what I see you doing
You're beautiful just as you are!

I love you Char Cakes!

I hope you enjoyed the book; please follow me on Facebook at **Poet L Joy Stevens**. You will get to read poems and stay updated on new books when they become available. Also, please support me on Amazon.com by purchasing and leaving your comments. This is greatly appreciated.

Thank you for your support!

L Joy Stevens

Made in the USA
Charleston, SC
30 November 2014